by Samantha Montgomery
illustrated by Susan Frankenberry

SCHOOL PUBLISHERS

Copyright © by Harcourt, Inc.

Printed in China

ISBN 10: 0-15-358447-5
ISBN 13: 978-0-15-358447-3

Ordering Options
ISBN 10: 0-15-358357-6 (Grade K Above-Level Collection)
ISBN 13: 978-0-15-358357-5 (Grade K Above-Level Collection)
ISBN 10: 0-15-360684-3 (package of 5)
ISBN 13: 978-0-15-360684-7 (package of 5)

5 6 7 8 9 10 985 15 14 13 12 11 10 09

I want to go out.
It will be fun in the snow.

I will get my coat.
Dad will get my hat for me.

Dad will zip it up for me.
He will zip his coat.

Dad and I will go out.
We will have fun in the snow.

Dad and I see a big hill.
We will go up to the top.

I will come down.
Dad will come down.

Dad and I have fun!